ILLUSTRATIONS BY JENNY MY DUBET

JERICO MANDYBUR

DAILY ORACLE

SEEK ANSWERS FROM YOUR HIGHER SELF

Hardie Grant

BOOKS

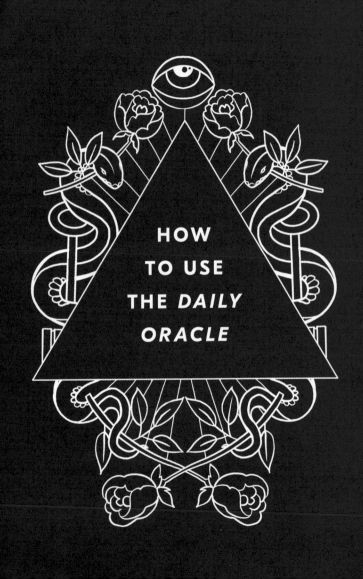

HOW
TO USE
THE *DAILY*
ORACLE

Respect and cherish the Oracle (and your higher self) by asking one thoughtful question every day.

1. Breathe deeply for three counts, holding the closed book next to your heart.

2. Quiet your mind and focus on your question. See the question in your mind's eye or say it aloud.

3. Run a finger along all the page edges and when you feel called, stop and open the book in that place. This is your higher self's answer to your question.

4. Trust what you've read and consider how it relates to your question and your energy right now.

MEET YOUR HIGHER SELF

Each of us has a 'higher self' deep inside us. It's the essence of who we are, or who we were before the world got to us. Before social conditioning; before we decided we were separate from the universe; before we stopped listening to our intuition. Before we had fear and only knew love.

Your higher self is *you*. It's the you that's still connected to all consciousness. It's the synchronistic you. The magical you that exists across time and space, and will always continue to — more your soul than your mind. And while your brain-chatter might shout, your higher self whispers. This book is an exercise in quiet — so you can learn to hear it.

When taking the time to ask the *Daily Oracle* a question, you slow down and hold space for the sacredness in the present moment so your higher self can step forward and provide an answer. Remember, the *Oracle* is revealing, but it's *you* who really holds the answers — they can only be found within your own interpretations. Trust that each answer you receive is perfect for you, right where you are at this moment. And when receiving them, always know: you are in control of your own life.

Some of the answers the *Oracle* will bring you are pithy. Some are easily understood. Others will make you re-examine what you thought you knew about the question you asked. Some will provide you with affirmations that'll help you through. All are channeled — from my higher self, to yours — from a place of love, in the spirit of empowerment. They're designed to make you stop, breathe and reflect, allowing sacred truths into your mind and heart.

xo Jerico Mandybur

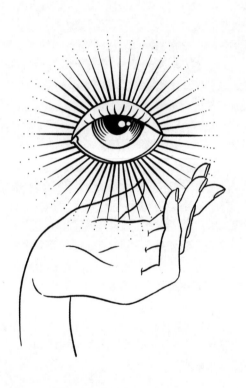

WOULD
YOU
RATHER
MAKE
MISTAKES,
OR
COLLECT
REGRETS?

THERE'S NOTHING WRONG WITH FAILING. YOU SHOULD TRY IT!

FLOWERS

DON'T CARE

WHO'S

WATCHING,

THEY JUST

BLOOM.

YOU
CAN'T
TAKE
YOUR
STUFF
WITH
YOU
WHEN
IT'S
OVER.

STOP.

WORRYING.

SO.

MUCH.

REAL PROGRESS REQUIRES YOU TO RETRACE YOUR STEPS.

POSSIBILITY

IS INFINITELY

REPRODUCTIVE.

TRUE JOY IS MULTIFACETED; FULL OF SHADE AS MUCH AS LIGHT.

YOU'RE ENTITLED TO ALL OF THE PEACE AND MORE.

IT'S TIME TO SAY GOODBYE TO WHAT DOESN'T SERVE YOU ANYMORE.

EXERCISING

EMPATHY MEANS

NOT THROWING

YOUR WEIGHT

AROUND.

STAY

AWAY.

UNHAPPY

PEOPLE LASH

OUT AT THOSE

THEY SEE

THEMSELVES

IN MOST.

**SHIELD
YOURSELF
FROM
NEGATIVITY
RIGHT
NOW.**

QUESTIONING EVERYTHING IS A SPIRITUAL ACT.

DON'T COUNT ON CERTAIN OUTCOMES INSTEAD OF RELYING ON YOUR OWN DAMN SELF.

YOU'RE
NOT FOR
EVERYONE.
YOU'RE
FOR YOU,
AND THE
PEOPLE
WHO
GET YOU.

AS HARD

AS IT IS,

KEEP GOING.

IT'S WORTH IT.

FIND
A QUIET
PLACE TO
MEDITATE.
YOU'LL BE
AMAZED
AT WHAT
CAN
COME UP.

LET
YOUR
MOST
WILD,
MESSY
SELF
EMERGE.

YOUR SPIRIT GUIDES HAVE GOT YOUR BACK.

NO ONE EVER GOT ANYWHERE BY GIVING A F*CK ABOUT WHAT OTHER PEOPLE THINK.

NOBODY KNOWS WHAT THEY'RE DOING. DON'T LET THAT STOP YOU.

THERE'S

NOTHING LONELY

ABOUT STANDING

ON YOUR OWN

TWO FEET.

TIME ONLY HAS THE MEANING AND STRUCTURE WE GIVE IT.

YOUR ONLY

TASK IS

TO KNOW

THYSELF.

SOFTNESS

IS THE MOST

REBELLIOUS

EXPRESSION

OF STRENGTH.

WAIT
FOR
PERMISSION,
AND
YOU'LL
BE
WAITING
FOREVER.

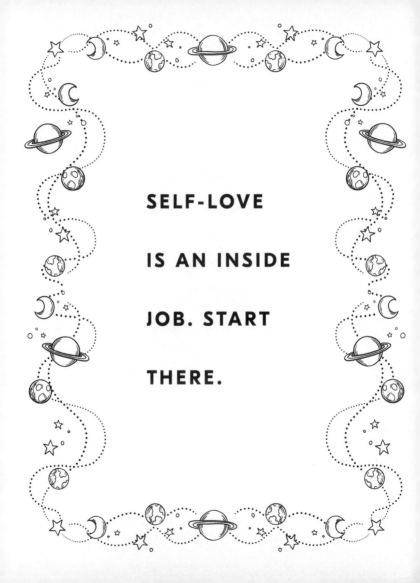

SELF-LOVE

IS AN INSIDE

JOB. START

THERE.

IF YOU
CAN
DREAM
IT, YOU
CAN
MAKE
IT
HAPPEN.

NO ONE
IS PURE
ANGEL
OR PURE
JERK.
WE'RE
ALL BOTH.

HARVEST

WHAT SERVES

YOU AND LET

THE REST

GO TO SEED.

CONSOLIDATE YOUR POWER INSTEAD OF SPREADING IT THIN.

ONLY YOU CAN EVER HOPE TO HEAL YOURSELF — NO ONE ELSE.

GROUND

YOURSELF.

REFUSE TO BE

DEFINED BY YOUR

CIRCUMSTANCES.

YOU'RE WORTHY OF ALL THE LOVE YOU DESIRE AND YOU HAVE THE POWER TO SHOW YOURSELF THAT LOVE NOW.

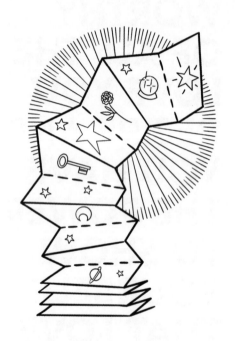

ALLOW THINGS TO UNFOLD.

NO ONE IS RESPONSIBLE FOR THE WAY YOU REACT BUT YOU.

BE SMART WITH

YOUR HEART.

YOU ARE THE

STEWARD OF

YOUR EMOTIONAL

WELL-BEING.

YOU HAVE THE ABILITY TO CREATE WONDERFUL THINGS. DON'T WASTE IT.

YOU ARE
A CHILD
OF LOVE,
CONNECTED
TO ALL
SPACE
AND TIME.

PRODUCTIVITY

ISN'T

EVERYTHING.

FOCUS ON PROTECTING YOUR ENERGY BEFORE YOU WORRY ABOUT ANYTHING ELSE.

PUT YOUR TRUST IN DIVINE TIMING.

EMBRACE YOUR

'FLAWS' AND

LOVE THEM.

WE DON'T NEED TO COMPREHEND OUR HIGHER POWER'S PLAN FOR US. WE JUST NEED TO ALLOW IT.

DON'T LET

ANYONE NEG

YOU, OR MAKE

YOU FEEL

SMALL.

THESE OLD STORIES AREN'T YOURS ANYMORE. WRITE YOURSELF A NEW FUTURE.

YOU
WOULDN'T
BE
THINKING IT
IF IT WASN'T
POSSIBLE.

YOU ARE NOT STUCK. GET UP AND WALK AWAY.

DON'T STAY SO LONG EXPLORING YOUR INNER WORLD THAT YOU'RE TRAPPED THERE.

START WITH A

STRONG SPIRITUAL

FOUNDATION,

AND THE REST

WILL BUILD ITSELF.

SHH, THERE'S NOTHING TO FIGHT OR FLY FROM NOW.

SOMETIMES

WHAT WE

WANT TO WANT

ISN'T WHAT WE

ACTUALLY WANT.

STOP

DAYDREAMING

AND START

DOING.

SLOW DOWN! MULTI-TASKING USUALLY MEANS DOING MORE THAN ONE THING, BADLY.

NURTURE YOURSELF LIKE A BABY.

YOU'RE RIGHT WHERE YOU'RE MEANT TO BE.

TURN THE VOLUME

DOWN ON YOUR

MIND SO YOU

CAN HEAR YOUR

INNER VOICE'S

LI'L WHISPER.

WHY TAKE ONE STEP, WHEN YOU COULD START RUNNING?

TRUST

YOUR

GUT.

SEEK AND YE SHALL FIND.

YOU DESERVE DIGNITY AND RESPECT. JUST LIKE EVERYONE ELSE.

**LET GO
OF YOUR
QUESTIONS.
EMBRACE
NOT
KNOWING.**

NEGATIVE

THOUGHTS ARE

NOT *YOU.*

DON'T MISTAKE

THEM FOR YOUR

REALITY.

WHAT IF YOU REALISED HOW POWERFUL YOU REALLY WERE?

STOP. NOTICE HOW YOU'RE FEELING, FIRST.

THERE ARE PEOPLE AROUND YOU WHO CARE A LOT. SEE THEM.

**GO CUDDLE
A TREE.**
SERIOUSLY.

YOUR

EXPERIENCE

IS

VALID.

THERE'S NOTHING WRONG WITH A *FEW* DELUSIONS OF GRANDEUR.

DON'T EVER LET YOUR CONDUCT BETRAY YOUR CAUSE.

GIVE YOURSELF

CONSENT TO

SIMPLY EXIST.

EVERYBODY'S JUST DOING THEIR BEST, BB.

BE PATIENT. GOING SLOW DOESN'T MEAN YOU'RE NOT GOING.

YOU ALREADY KNOW EXACTLY HOW TO BE. TRUST.

YOU

ANSWER

TO

NO ONE.

IMPOSTOR SYNDROME IS KINDA UNIVERSAL. DON'T STRESS ABOUT IT.

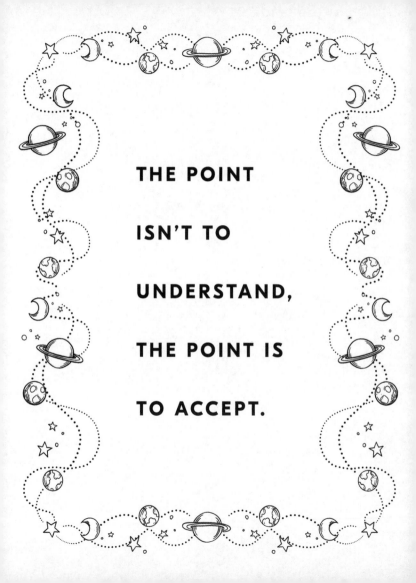

THE POINT
ISN'T TO
UNDERSTAND,
THE POINT IS
TO ACCEPT.

TAKE A
PAUSE TO
RECUPERATE
BEFORE
YOU DO
ANYTHING.

MIND YOUR OWN BUSINESS BEFORE YOU STICK YOUR NECK INTO OTHER'S.

DO YOU *REALLY* CARE

MORE ABOUT THE

DESTINATION THAN

ALL THAT TIME SPENT

ON THE JOURNEY?

SEE THE GOOD. ACKNOWLEDGE WHAT YOU HAVE.

COMPARISON

IS A TRICKY

BITCH.

YOU
ARE
NOT
WHAT
THEY
SAY
YOU
ARE.

LET GO,

OR BE

DRAGGED.

'HOME' IS
WHEREVER
THE HELL
YOU WANT
IT TO BE.

THE UNIVERSE IS NOT A PIE. THERE'S MORE THAN ENOUGH TO GO AROUND.

EVERYTHING HAS BEEN LEADING UP TO THIS MOMENT.

STEP ONE IS

UNPACKING

THAT

QUESTION

YOURSELF.

YOU'RE BEING TESTED. STEP UP AND HONOUR YOUR TRUTH.

YOUR SENSITIVITY IS YOUR SUPERPOWER.

ONE THING AT A TIME AND *WHEN* IT'S TIME.

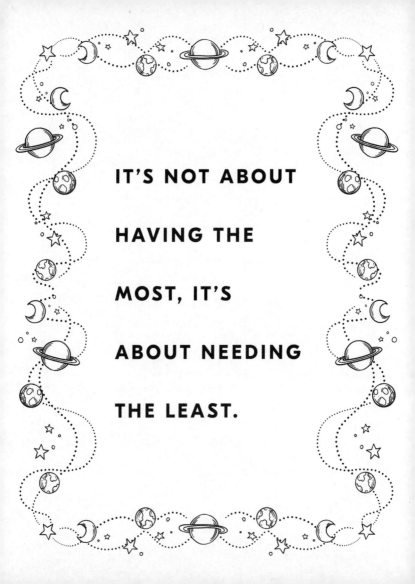

IT'S NOT ABOUT HAVING THE MOST, IT'S ABOUT NEEDING THE LEAST.

SELF-CARE

MEANS

TENDING TO

YOUR MOST

BASIC NEEDS

FIRST.

WHY IS IT SO HARD TO SHOW YOURSELF THE LOVE YOU SHOW OTHERS?

YOU'D BE

SURPRISED.

STOP. THE ANSWERS YOU'RE CRAVING ARE FOUND IN STILLNESS.

YOU ARE

PROTECTED.

YOU'LL GET OUT EXACTLY WHAT YOU PUT IN.

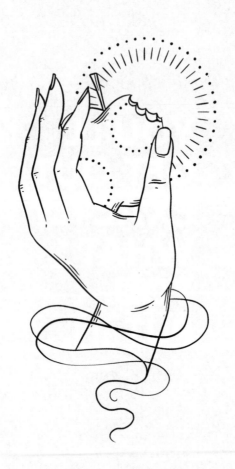

DON'T EXPECT TO EAT THE FRUIT IF YOU'VE ONLY JUST PLANTED THE SEED.

LOOSEN

YOUR

GRIP.

THE OUTCOME IS NOT THE POINT.

YOU ARE WORTHY OF MUCH MORE.

SEARCH YOUR HEART. YOU'LL KNOW WHAT TO DO WHEN THE TIME COMES.

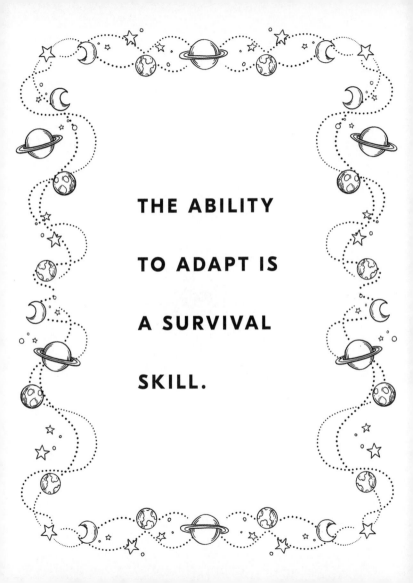

THE ABILITY

TO ADAPT IS

A SURVIVAL

SKILL.

ALIGN YOURSELF TO WHAT YOUR SPIRIT ALREADY KNOWS YOU DESERVE.

DON'T BE

FOOLED.

THIS ISN'T

WHERE IT

ENDS.

IN
EVERY
INSTANCE,
CHOOSE
LOVE
OVER
FEAR.

LET.

IT.

GO.

THIS IS THE SIGN YOU'VE BEEN WAITING FOR.

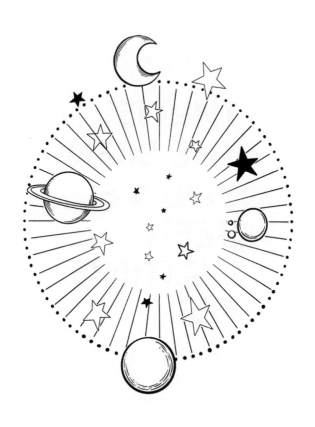

SAY 'YES' AND THE UNIVERSE WILL ECHO IT BACK TO YOU.

IT'S TIME

TO GET

TO WORK.

PATIENCE IS A

SKILL YOU'LL

NEVER REGRET

MASTERING.

YOUR EGO IS NOT IN CHARGE, YOUR SPIRIT IS. LISTEN TO THAT INSTEAD.

STOP

PLAYING

SMALL.

NOT EVERYTHING IS WHAT IT SEEMS.

GOETHE WAS ON TO SOMETHING WHEN HE SAID 'DOUBT ONLY GROWS WITH KNOWLEDGE'.

**THERE'S
NO
HONOUR
LIKE BEING
HUMBLED
BEFORE THE
MYSTERIES
OF LIFE.**

IF YOU KNEW

THE ANSWER,

THERE WOULD

BE NO LESSON.

DON'T FEED THE TROLLS IN YOUR HEAD.

THE
PAST
IS IN
THE
PAST.

YOU'RE STRONGER THAN YOU REALISE.

ABSOLUTELY.

FOCUSING ON YOUR SUPPOSED 'DEFECTS' IS A FORM OF EMOTIONAL SELF-ABUSE.

DON'T

WEAPONISE

YOUR

GENEROSITY.

IF
EVERYONE
ELSE
JUMPED
OFF A
BRIDGE,
WOULD
YOU DO
IT?

WITHOUT FAILURE, WE WOULD NEVER LEARN.

MOVE

FORWARD

WITH

GRACE.

IF YOU CAN'T FORGIVE THEM, AT LEAST FORGIVE YOURSELF.

SEEING YOURSELF

THROUGH SOMEONE

ELSE'S EYES IS

ILLUMINATING.

SELF-LOVE IS THE FOUNTAIN FROM WHICH ALL OTHER LOVES SPRING.

SIT STILL,

AND

LISTEN.

WHAT IF THE STUFF YOU WANT TO MANIFEST, YOU HAD ACCESS TO ALL ALONG?

BREATHE IN DEEPLY

THROUGH YOUR

NOSE, FEELING YOUR

BELLY EXPAND. HOLD

FOR THREE COUNTS.

EXHALE FULLY

THROUGH YOUR

MOUTH. REPEAT.

EVERYTHING IS GOING TO BE JUST FINE.

**TRUE
FREEDOM
IS
NOT BEING
ATTACHED
TO THE
OUTCOME.**

DON'T COUNT YOUR CHICKENS, CHICKEN.

LOOKING BACK SO OFTEN WON'T PROPEL YOU FORWARD.

'LACK' IS A CONSTRUCT THAT WOULD SEE US DEPRIVE OTHERS.

NOTHING IS MISSING FROM YOUR LIFE THAT YOU CAN'T REPLACE YOURSELF.

IT'S NOT
THAT
SERIOUS,
HONEY.
RELAX.

DON'T

STOP

BELIEVING.

YOU CAN ONLY

DO SOMETHING

WELL IF YOU'RE

WILLING TO DO

IT POORLY FIRST.

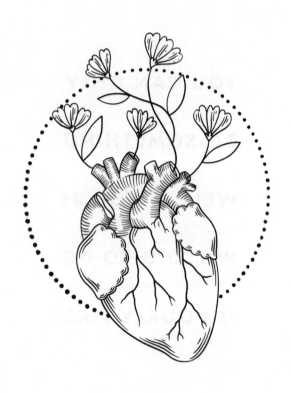

IGNORE YOUR HEAD FOR A SECOND. WHAT DOES YOUR HEART SAY?

YOU CAN

(AND SHOULD)

DO BETTER.

STOP THINKING SO MUCH, AND LET YOURSELF *FEEL.*

BE CAREFUL WITH

YOUR EMOTIONS.

USE TEMPERANCE.

TELL THE WHOLE TRUTH, ALWAYS.

DON'T IGNORE THE BIGGER PICTURE.

WHAT YOU CAN'T STAND IN OTHERS IS AN UNRESOLVED PART OF YOU.

LIFE IS A SPIRAL

STAIRCASE. YOU

WILL CONFRONT

THIS AGAIN AND

AGAIN, WISER

EACH TIME.

BE STRATEGIC, NOT ALL-OUT SNEAKY.

YOUR ANCESTORS ARE WATCHING OVER YOU.

IMAGINE A LIFE FULL OF 'WHAT IFS'. NOW, DO THE THING.

IF YOU'RE LOOKING FOR OPPORTUNITIES, CREATE THEM.

DECEITFUL PEOPLE DON'T GET YOUR ATTENTION ANYMORE.

CONVICTION

IS A LIGHT

THAT CAN

NEVER BE

BLOWN OUT.

YOU ARE

THE ONLY

PERSON

WHO CAN

REALLY

STOP YOU.

THE NOISE IN YOUR HEAD ISN'T HELPING ANYMORE. SEE IT FOR WHAT IT IS.

DON'T

GILD

THE

LILY.

WHAT WOULD

[INSERT YOUR

FAV SPIRITUAL

REVOLUTIONARY]

DO?

HOLD YOUR VISION TOO TIGHTLY AND YOU RISK SMOTHERING IT.

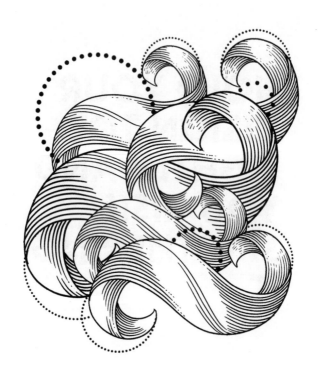

INTENSITY IS A

WAVE YOU CAN

RIDE, ELATED —

OR IT CAN WIPE

YOU OUT.

USE BALANCE.

DON'T SEEK IN OTHERS WHAT YOU CAN FIND IN YOURSELF.

NOTHING

WORTHWHILE

IS EASY.

IF IT DOESN'T FEEL RIGHT TODAY, IT WON'T FEEL RIGHT TOMORROW.

IF YOU WANT THE TRUTH, SIMPLY STRIP AWAY EVERY ILLUSION.

STAY

IN YOUR

OWN

LANE.

DON'T CHANGE

YOUR DREAMS,

CHANGE THE

WAY YOU'RE

GOING TO

REACH THEM.

THE BEST RELATIONSHIPS ARE WITH PEOPLE THAT TEACH US MORE ABOUT OURSELVES.

SOMETHING BIG IS COMING. YOUR ACTIONS WILL HELP DETERMINE WHAT IT IS.

IT'S A CLICHÉ
BECAUSE
IT'S TRUE —
YOU NEED
TO FOLLOW
YOUR HEART.

IF YOU
DON'T
EXAMINE
YOUR
WOUNDS,
HOW
CAN YOU
EXPECT
TO CLEAN
THEM?

BE GENTLE.
YOU'RE
PRECIOUS
CARGO.

SETTLE THE

STORMS IN

YOUR MIND,

THEN ASK

AGAIN WHEN

YOU'RE REALLY

LISTENING.

BE A

SPONGE.

LEARN.

**STAND
IN YOUR
POWER.**

**YOU ARE
STRONG.**

**YOU ARE
SOVEREIGN.**

FOR BETTER OR WORSE, THE SQUEAKY WHEEL GETS THE GREASE.

ACKNOWLEDGE

YOUR STORY AS

YOUR OWN, SO

YOU CAN START

WRITING IT FOR

YOURSELF.

CLEANSE YOURSELF AND YOUR SPACE.

NOBODY OWES YOU ANYTHING. SO WHAT DO YOU OWE YOURSELF?

EVERYONE HAS A SHADOW SELF. BE WILLING TO PEEK AT YOURS, AND YOU'LL LEARN A LOT.

YOU CAN

BE YOUR

HARSHEST

CRITIC, OR

YOUR OWN

BEST FRIEND.

CHOOSE.

YOU'LL CROSS THAT BRIDGE WHEN YOU COME TO IT.

PAIN IS BEING

SLAPPED IN

THE FACE BY

CONSCIOUSNESS.

YOU'RE AWAKE.

ALL SIGNS

POINT TO

'YES'.

SHOW
UP FOR
YOURSELF,
SO YOU
CAN SHOW
UP FOR
OTHERS.

IF YOU 'DON'T KNOW', JUST COMMIT TO FIGURING IT OUT. IT'S NOT ROCKET SCIENCE.

**DON'T
LISTEN
TO
PEOPLE
WHO
EXPLAIN
WHO *YOU*
ARE.**

IT'S OKAY TO IMPROVISE.

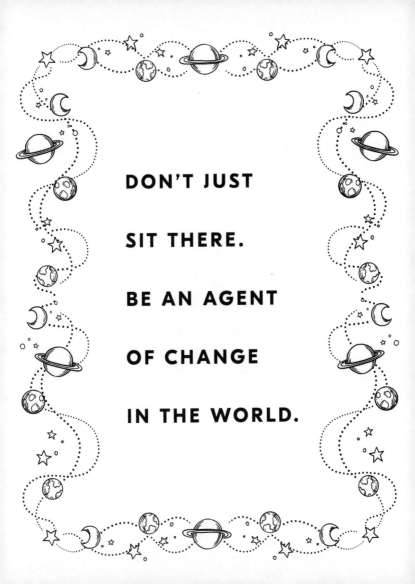

DON'T JUST

SIT THERE.

BE AN AGENT

OF CHANGE

IN THE WORLD.

IF YOU WEREN'T DEALING WITH THIS, YOU WOULDN'T BE HUMAN.

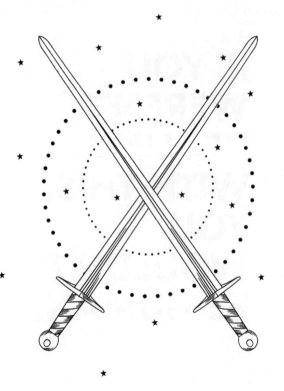

YOU HAVE EVERY RIGHT TO STAND UP FOR YOURSELF.

THE MORE

YOU KNOW,

THE LESS

YOU NEED.

YOU DON'T NEED TO HAVE EVERYTHING FIGURED OUT ALL THE TIME.

YOUR WILL IS

YOUR MOST

POWERFUL TOOL.

BE RESPONSIBLE

WITH HOW YOU

WIELD IT.

WHAT DOESN'T SERVE YOU IS SLOWING YOU DOWN.

SOMETIMES, IT'S NOT ABOUT YOU.

'IT'S A YES FROM ME' — THE UNIVERSE

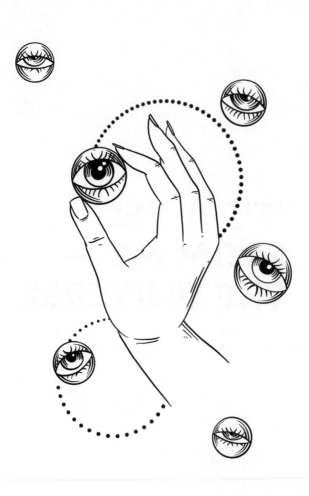

CAN YOU SEE YOURSELF THROUGH THEIR EYES?

TO DOUBT IS A

SPIRITUAL ACT.

YOU
CAN
MAKE
SOMETHING
OUT
OF
NOTHING.

OPEN THE

F*CK UP.

LOOK

BEFORE

YOU

LEAP.

WHEN WE'RE TESTED IS WHEN WE REVEAL OUR TRUEST SELVES.

SELF-BELIEF IS THE KEY TO ANY FORM OF MOTIVATION.

WHEN YOU'RE CAUGHT BETWEEN A ROCK AND A HARD PLACE, JUST WIGGLE OUT.

PEOPLE ARE

CONSTANTLY

TELLING YOU WHO

THEY REALLY ARE.

PAY ATTENTION.

IF YOU WOULDN'T WANT IT FOR YOUR BEST FRIEND, DON'T ACCEPT IT FOR YOURSELF.

WHAT DRAINS YOU IRREDEEMABLY HAS NO BUSINESS HERE.

EVERYBODY

FEELS THIS

WAY.

'TOMORROW'
IS THE PERFECT
EXCUSE
BECAUSE IT
NEVER COMES.

THE SPIRITUAL IS PERSONAL AND THE PERSONAL IS POLITICAL.

THE HIGHER POWER IS *YOU.*

THE MEANING

OF LIFE IS

WHATEVER

YOU BRING

TO IT.

SEE THE GOOD IN THE WORLD, AND RECEIVE IT.

GETTING WHAT YOU WANT MEANS NOTHING IF YOU GAVE AWAY YOUR INTEGRITY.

ALCHEMISE WHAT'S IN FRONT OF YOU INTO SOMETHING ELSE.

HALF-ARSED EFFORTS YIELD HALF-ARSED RESULTS.

THERE'S

NO SHAME

IN SHINING.

DON'T SWEAT THE MINOR DETAILS WHEN THERE'S A BIG PICTURE TO ABSORB.

STOP LOOKING FOR VALIDATION AND SURRENDER TO WHAT IS.

YOU

ARE

LOVED.

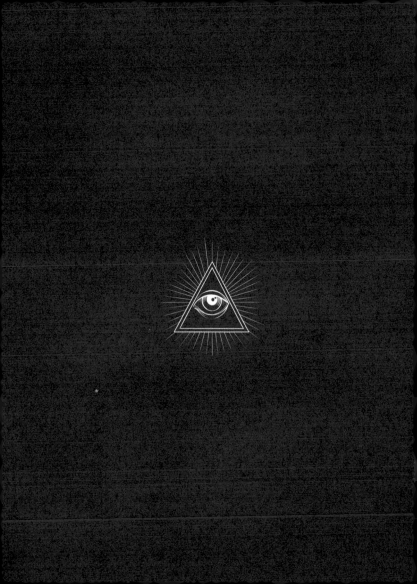

LIFE IS A SCHOOL.

DON'T BE ONE OF

THOSE KIDS WHO

THINKS THEY

ALREADY KNOW

EVERYTHING.

HOLD SPACE FOR YOUR HEART.

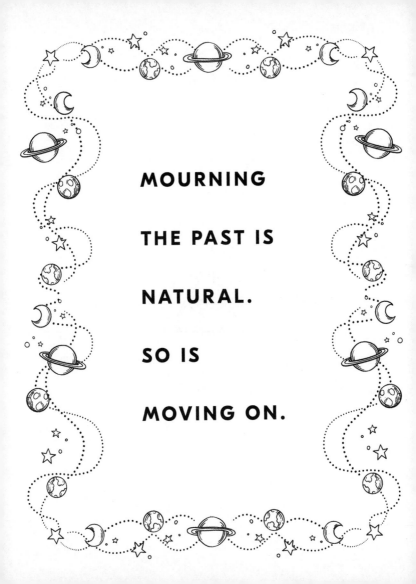

MOURNING

THE PAST IS

NATURAL.

SO IS

MOVING ON.

BETTER LATE THAN NEVER, SWEETIE.

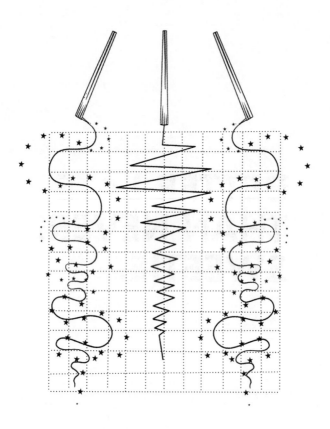

FIRE UP THE BULLSH*T DETECTOR AND SEE THINGS FOR WHAT THEY ARE.

YOU HAVE
EVERYTHING
IT TAKES TO
DIG DEEP.

'NORMAL' IS A SETTING ON THE DRYER.

BE RECEPTIVE TO

WHAT'S BEING

OFFERED TO YOU.

FAUX-VULNERABILITY IS A THING. MAKE YOURS REAL.

EVERYTHING

IN

MODERATION.

THE BUMPER STICKERS WERE RIGHT: MAGIC DOES HAPPEN.

EVERYONE HAS A STORY. SHARE YOURS AND LISTEN TO THEIRS.

THEIR INSECURITIES ARE NOT *YOUR* REALITY.

THERE HAS ONLY EVER BEEN, AND WILL ONLY EVER BE, ONE YOU.

YOU'RE

NOT READY

TO KNOW.

THERE'S NO SUCH THING AS A FREE LUNCH.

COMMIT TO

YOURSELF

WHOLEHEARTEDLY

AND YOU'LL NEVER

BE LONELY.

YOUR JOY IS CONTAGIOUS. FIND IT AND SHARE IT.

LIFE
ITSELF IS A
CHALLENGE.
RISE TO IT.

LITTLE

BY

LITTLE.

WHAT'S IN YOUR SOUL HAS A RIGHT TO SHINE THROUGH YOU.

IT'S TRUE
WHAT THEY
SAY ABOUT
NOT JUDGING
A BOOK BY
ITS COVER.

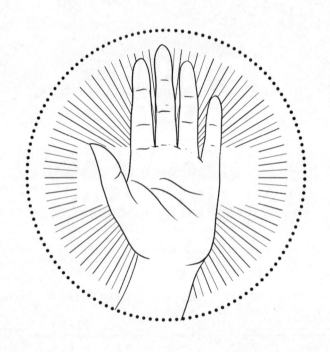

YOU
CAN
STOP.
YOU
KNOW
YOU
CAN.

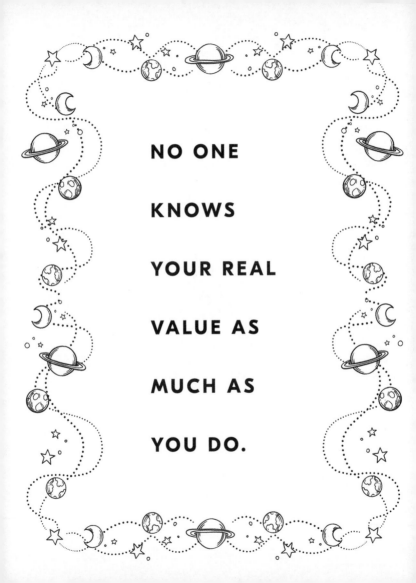

NO ONE

KNOWS

YOUR REAL

VALUE AS

MUCH AS

YOU DO.

JUSTICE

WILL

BE

SERVED.

'SUCCESS'
IS JUST AN
ABSTRACT
WORD
THAT NO
ONE EVER
RELATES TO.

THINK ABOUT WHAT YOU THINK YOU WANT VERY CAREFULLY.

I'M NOT AN EIGHT

BALL. TAKE YOUR

QUESTION MORE

SERIOUSLY, FOCUS,

AND ASK AGAIN.

STOP SWEATING

THE THINGS THAT

DON'T MATTER AND

PAY ATTENTION TO

THE ONES THAT DO.

DISCIPLINE IS AN ESSENTIAL PART OF CREATIVITY AND GROWTH.

IT'S CLOSER THAN YOU THINK.

PUT

YOURSELF

FIRST.

THERE ARE A LOT OF THINGS WE CAN'T SEE. DOESN'T MAKE THEM LESS TRUE.

WHEN YOU SEE

HOW MANY

PEOPLE HOLD

SH*TTY OPINIONS,

YOU REALISE

POPULARITY

MEANS NOTHING.

YOU CAN'T SEE

IN FRONT OF YOU

WHEN YOU'RE

CARRYING SUCH

A LARGE BURDEN

AROUND. DROP IT.

WHO CARES HOW LONG IT TAKES?

YOU ARE SO MUCH MORE THAN YOUR OUTPUT.

WE ALL
SHARE
THE SAME
PURPOSE;
TO LOVE
AND
TO BE
LOVED.

SOMETIMES
THERE'S
NOTHING
YOU NEED
TO DO
BUT REST.

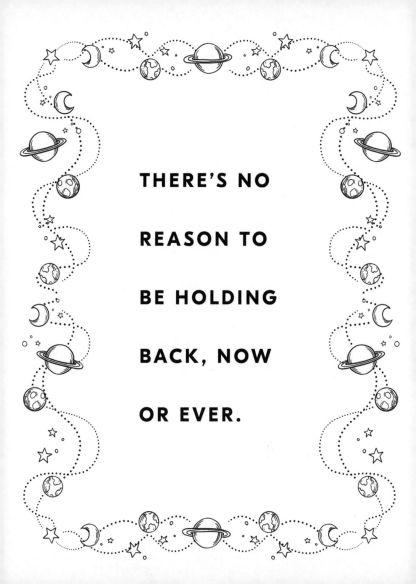

THERE'S NO REASON TO BE HOLDING BACK, NOW OR EVER.

MATERIAL THINGS ARE NOT THE MEASURE OF A PERSON.

THE PARTS OF OURSELVES WE AVOID ARE WHERE THE GEMS LIE.

WAS
IT
EVER
TRULY
YOURS
TO
BEGIN
WITH?

NOT EVERYONE WILL

UNDERSTAND YOUR

WORTH, THAT'S WHY

IT'S CRUCIAL YOU DO.

GRATITUDE

IS

EVERYTHING.

SAY 'NOT TODAY SATAN' AND MOVE ON.

DON'T BE AFRAID TO OPEN YOUR EYES TO WHAT'S ALREADY IN FRONT OF YOU, LOVE.

LIFE HAS
A WAY OF
MIRRORING
BACK TO
YOU WHAT
NEEDS
ADDRESSING.

EASY COME,

EASY GO.

IS IT
IN THE
BEST
INTERESTS
OF ALL
INVOLVED?

SET FIRMER BOUNDARIES. LET ONLY THE BEST THINGS PASS THROUGH.

SHAKE

IT OUT,

LITERALLY.

GET YOUR

ENERGY

FLOWING.

DON'T EXPECT ANYTHING WITHOUT *DOING* ANYTHING.

GETTING INTO

NATURE IS THE

QUICKEST WAY

TO CLEAR YOUR

HEAD. AND YOU

SHOULD.

**GUILT IS
A USELESS
EMOTION
WITH ZERO
REDEEMING
QUALITIES.**

YOU ARE A SHAPESHIFTER. ALLOW YOURSELF TO TRANSFORM.

HOWEVER

DAUNTING

THE QUESTION,

COMMUNICATION

IS ALWAYS

THE ANSWER.

YOUR PASSION WILL GET YOU EVERYWHERE.

THEY DON'T CALL IT

'DOING THE WORK'

BECAUSE IT'S EASY.

WORK WITH — NOT AGAINST — THE PEOPLE AROUND YOU NOW.

VISUALISE WHAT YOU WANT, AND THEN MAKE SURE IT COMES TRUE.

YOU WON'T UNDERSTAND UNTIL YOU FULLY EXPERIENCE.

CHERISH

WHAT'S

YOURS

AND

RESPECT

THEIRS.

KINDNESS SOMETIMES MEANS SAYING 'NO'.

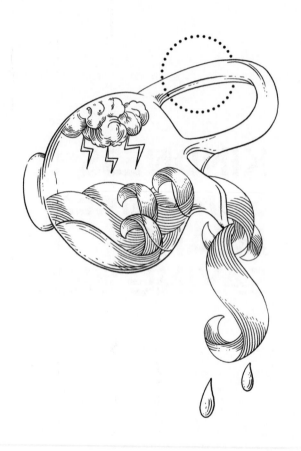

YOUR ANGER IS RIGHTEOUS. TAKE A SIP AND LET IT FUEL YOU, BUT DON'T GUZZLE ITS POISON.

WHY SO

HASTY?

THINK

ABOUT IT.

WHEN YOU'RE

OVERLY ATTACHED

TO HOW THINGS

ARE, THE CONSTANT

NATURE OF CHANGE

IS TORTURE.

IS THAT THE TRUTH, OR JUST A STORY YOU HEARD?

**YOUR
INTUITION
IS THE
GREATEST
GIFT YOU
HAVE.
USE IT.**

NO ONE CAN SEE WHAT YOU'RE FEELING. THEY CAN ONLY SEE YOUR ACTIONS.

THERE'S NO NEED TO LEAVE ANYTHING TO CHANCE.

IT IS
WHAT
IT IS.

DON'T NEGLECT

YOUR NEED

FOR DEEP

CONNECTIONS.

YOU ARE A

SOCIAL BEING.

IT TAKES BRAVERY TO BE AUTHENTIC. BE THAT GUY.

YOU DON'T HAVE

TO TOLERATE BEING

ASKED TO PERFORM

INSTEAD OF JUST

BEING ACCEPTED

AS YOU ARE.

EVERY THOUGHT IS A SPELL. CAST THE RIGHT ONES.

YOUR

POTENTIAL

IS ENDLESS.

SURRENDER TO

THE FACT THAT

NO ONE HAS ALL

THE ANSWERS.

NOT EVEN CLOSE.

**BLESSINGS
ON
BLESSINGS.**

LIGHTEN YOUR EMOTIONAL LOAD AND YOU'LL SEE THINGS MORE CLEARLY.

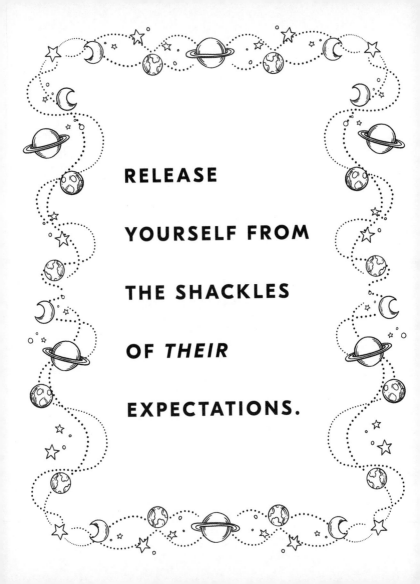

RELEASE

YOURSELF FROM

THE SHACKLES

OF *THEIR*

EXPECTATIONS.

YOUR BODY IS A TEMPLE. TREAT IT LIKE THE SACRED THING IT IS.

ABUNDANCE IS A STATE OF MIND.

MY

SOURCES

SAY NO.

YOU CAN'T

TAKE BACK

WHAT'S COME

TO PASS BUT

YOU CAN

CHANGE HOW

YOU THINK

ABOUT IT.

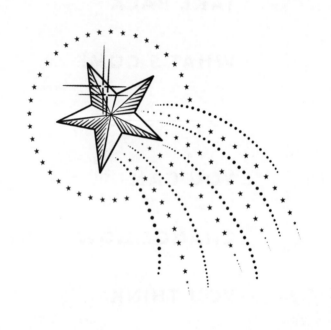

YOU
DON'T
EVER SEE
YOUR
NORTH
STAR,
YOU JUST
TRUST
YOU HAVE
ONE.

YOUR IMAGINATION IS A LEGITIMATE SOURCE OF KNOWLEDGE AND MEANING. BELIEVE.

THE QUICKEST WAY TO BE SERVED IS TO BE OF SERVICE.

NOW IS

THE TIME.

YOU CAN

DO IT!

YOU'RE NOT THE CENTRE OF EVERYTHING. SORRY.

IT'S OKAY IF YOU'RE SCARED, BUT YOU DEFINITELY DON'T NEED TO BE.

IS THIS REALLY A HILL YOU'RE WILLING TO DIE ON?

DO WHAT

YOU LOVE,

EVEN IF YOU

NEVER GET

PAID FOR IT.

YOU CAN'T

ALWAYS FIGHT

FIRE WITH FIRE.

WITH SOME,

YOU HAVE TO

JUST LET THEM

BURN OUT.

NOBODY
OWNS
OR
COMPLETES
YOU,
BUT YOU.

IT'S OKAY TO HIBERNATE. YOU'LL COME OUT STRONGER.

'CONTROL' IS AN

ILLUSION. NOTHING

IS UNDER CONTROL

AND THAT'S FINE.

**BEWARE
OF FALSE
PROPHETS.**

YOUR SHAME

IS NOT YOURS,

YOU'VE JUST

TAKEN IT ON.

LET IT GO NOW.

ASK FOR

A SIGN TO

APPEAR IN

A DREAM,

AND

YOU'LL SEE.

LET YOURSELF BE SEEN. TAKE UP SPACE.

THINGS ARE GOING TO HAPPEN, AND FAST. BE READY.

IT'S WHAT
YOU HAVE
(NOT WHAT
YOU DON'T
HAVE)
THAT'S
WORTH
THINKING
ABOUT.

NOW IS THE TIME

TO HARNESS ALL

THE POWERS OF

YOUR LOGIC AND

RATIONALITY.

GO
FOR IT!
JUST BE
SMART
ABOUT
IT.

'I LOVE YOU
SO MUCH
AND I'M
PROUD
OF YOU.
IT'S OKAY.' —
YOUR INNER
CHILD

NOBODY HAS A MONOPOLY ON THE TRUTH.

LOOK
IN THE
MIRROR.

FULLY
ACCEPT
YOURSELF.

GO LIVE
LIKE IT.

LET THE

GOD(ESS)

IN YOU

ACKNOWLEDGE

THE GOD(ESS)

IN THEM.

CHANGE YOUR PERSPECTIVE AND YOU'LL SEE THINGS MORE CLEARLY.

THIS IS A BATTLE YOU CAN WIN, SO MAKE SURE YOU'RE PLAYING FAIR.

YOU'LL
RISE AGAIN
(YEP, LIKE A
PHOENIX).

NOTHING

REALLY DIES,

IT'S JUST

TRANSMUTED.

STAYING HUMBLE IS THE FLIP SIDE OF BEING PROUD. YOU NEED BOTH.

THERE IS

MUCH MORE

OUT THERE

FOR YOU.

**YOU CAN
WITHSTAND
THE MOST
INTENSE OF
STORMS.**

IT'S OKAY TO NOT WANT THE SAME THINGS AS EVERYBODY ELSE.

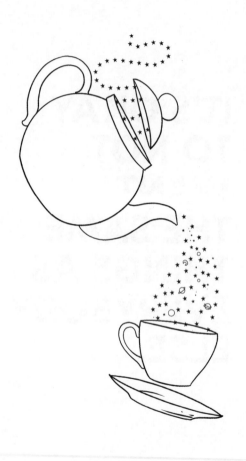

FIND THE
POETRY
IN THE
MUNDANE
AND
YOU'LL
ENJOY
YOURSELF
A LOT
MORE.

YOU

EARNED

IT,

BABE.

YOU
ALREADY
KNOW
THE
ANSWER.
TAKE TIME
AWAY TO
FIGURE IT
OUT.

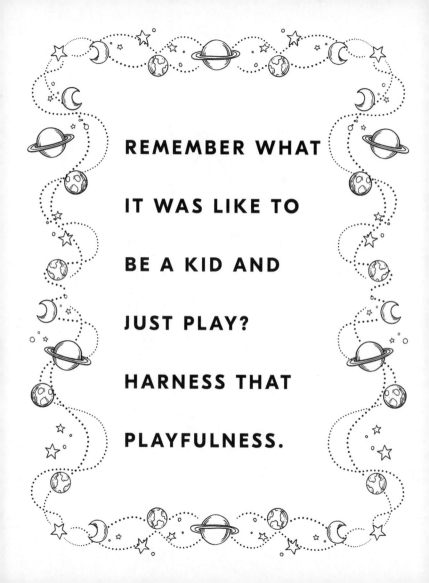

REMEMBER WHAT IT WAS LIKE TO BE A KID AND JUST PLAY? HARNESS THAT PLAYFULNESS.

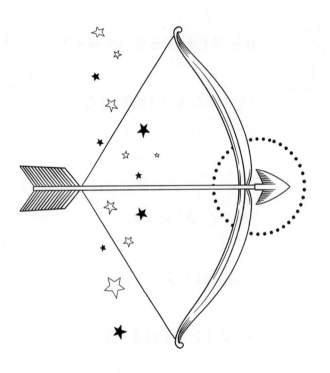

EMBODY THE WARRIOR. STEP INTO YOUR POWER.

DISTRACTIONS HAVE

A WAY OF MAKING

THEMSELVES LOOK

LIKE THE MOST

IMPORTANT THING.

YOU
CAN GET
THROUGH
THIS.
YOU'VE
GONE
THROUGH
WORSE.

YOUR IDEAS ARE

AMAZING AND

YOUR OPINIONS

VALID. DOESN'T

MEAN YOU DON'T

HAVE A LOT STILL

TO LEARN.

WHEN
THINGS
FALL APART,
IT'S A
CHANCE
TO PUT
THEM BACK
TOGETHER
IN A BETTER
WAY.

NOTHING

IS

PERMANENT.

NOTHING.

SEEK OUT MORE INFORMATION SO YOU CAN FORM YOUR OWN OPINION.

RECEIVE AS GENEROUSLY AS YOU GIVE.

THE BEST RELATIONSHIP WILL EXPOSE YOU AND BRING YOU BACK TO YOURSELF.

THE DARKEST PARTS OF YOURSELF ARE CRYING OUT FOR LOVE AND ACCEPTANCE.

**KEEP
YOUR
HEAD
DOWN
AND
STAY
OUT OF
TROUBLE.**

LET
WHAT
COMES,
COME.
LET
WHAT
GOES,
GO.

INSPIRATION IS

LIKE A MUSCLE.

IT TAKES DEDICATION

AND PRACTICE TO

LIFT YOUR SPIRITS.

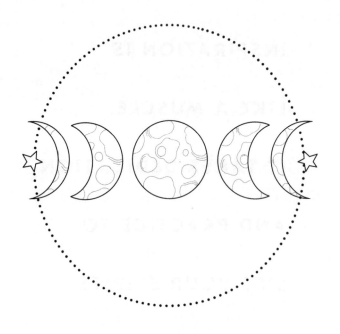

THE END
IS ALWAYS
JUST THE
BEGINNING
AGAIN.

SLOW

AND

STEADY,

BABY.